MACHINES LIKE US

MACHINES LIKE US

Joshua R. Helms

5220 Dexter Ann Arbor Rd.
Ann Arbor, MI 48103
www.dzancbooks.org

Designed by Steven Seighman
Cover photo by Lisa Tallin

Library of Congress Cataloging-in-Publication Data

Helms, Joshua R.
[Poems. Selections]
Machines like us / Joshua R. Helms.
pages cm
ISBN 978-1-938103-44-5 (paperback)
I. Title. PS3608.E39228A6 2016
811'.6—dc23

2015033338

First U.S. Edition: March 2016

Printed in the United States of America

10 9 8 7 6 5 4 3 2 1

CONTENTS

I

II

III

IV

The box is only temporary.

—Sylvia Plath

I

RESOLUTION

Historian, I keep having this dream where you & I are
machines: a metal fist overcome with daisy heads,
burnt stems collected around metal feet. The fist belongs
to a machine shaped like you & the feet belong to a machine
shaped like me. The you-machine closes its fist & opens its fist
& closes its fist & opens. I am programmed not to wince
at the sound of your hands. I am programmed to enjoy,
to show my metal teeth. Then the daisy heads are dust
& the dust looks like white pollen. It lifts into the air & settles
on my face. This makes me look human instead of machine.
I'm not sure what this means & you don't recognize
me. You are programmed to attack any moving body
that doesn't look like me & I know you designed this feature
because sometimes I am too gullible. But now I cannot
speak with you opening my metal chest with your metal
fingers. I'm not programmed to protect myself from you.
I would ask for rain at the expense of rust if I knew how.
But instead my wires are tangled in your metal fingers &
this is how we are for several days, my chest peeled & you
reaching inside until you're sure the wires are familiar.

RECORD

hard to tell whose mouth is

on whose body Boy's tattooed hip

obscured by shadow my beard

absent there is no way to tell us

apart there is no way to know

whose hand is at the camera

ESCAPE ATTEMPT

I'm burying photographs in the front yard flowerbed. The grass is topped with dew & stems are bent toward the pavement. Boy's dog is shitting next to the mailbox. Across the street our neighbors are having coffee on their porch. They ask how the lilies are doing & I wave & get into my car. In a few minutes Boy is going to wake up surrounded by open photo albums, every page a map of the yard with an X marking.

* * *

I drive into a tree near Boy's childhood home. My forehead bleeds when it meets the windshield. The hood sinks into the engine & my body crumples against the ground. The stereo continues to play a mix tape Boy made. After a few moments I'm able to get up. Boy's engraved Zippo is in my pocket with his initials. I light a map of Florida & toss it through the open window. The wind blows smoke into the trees & their leaves blacken. I unbutton my shirt for air. The road's quiet. I thumb anywhere that isn't Boy's direction.

* * *

I'm lying in the sand at the edge of another continent. My shirt is folded under my head & my belly is close to blistering. Boy nudges my body with his foot, drops a rubber-banded chunk of photographs on the sand. He sits beside me & disrupts my hair. He doesn't ask me why we're here, just says he has a room at a hotel & I can join him. We sit on the bed & look at our photographs. Boy rubs lotion on my sunburn. Dirt from our yard mixes in with sand from the beach. Boy takes a shower & when he comes to bed we watch a foreign film without subtitles. We manage to laugh at the right moments.

⋆ ⋆ ⋆

The day before we go home Boy & I are standing in the ocean. He's wearing this orange baseball cap he wore when we first met. His lips are against my peeling shoulder & my skin gets caught in his teeth. When we kiss, his hipbones puncture my hands. He tells me there's a stingray behind me. The water shifts & the sun turns white. Boy asks about the scar on my forehead. I tell him we are sweating each other out like fever. He says *I'm sorry I didn't get here sooner.*

DREAM

The grass is growing white
        from the dirt. The crab apple
trees are black. Our front door is red
        & Boy says I know this seems
like a bad piece of art, I know
        this seems like a movie
if only because it's visually stunning.
        The mailbox is rounded
against Boy's palm & he's opening
        & closing & opening & closing
with the other hand. The red flag is
        broken off at its stem. I'm trimming
the rose bushes. I turn to Boy & my hands
        are bloody & my lips are bloody.
When his mouth opens I slip him
        the thorns, each one carving
its tiny journey across our tongues.

EXPLORATION

Historian's body is bent over a pile of my

papers in our living room. He thinks I'm

still asleep in our bed. He doesn't know

Boy's hands are in the nightstand drawer.

He doesn't know that while he's looking

for answers I'm still asking more questions,

idly sliding Boy's fingers across my stomach,

remembering his ribs & teeth, the snow.

THIRD DATE

Boy opens the car door & a paper bag
empties. A scalpel stumbles into streetlight,
lands dead on the pavement. He collects
the instrument & deposits the bag
behind the front seat. Boy's cautious.
He sits me the same place the scalpel was
laying before he got here, says he's taking
me somewhere he's been before.

Boy opens my door, asks me to take a walk.
The scalpel flashes in his backpocket
& I follow him no matter that the woods
are obscure, that our shadows are blank
against the dirt. There's a tree picked out.
Boy's initialed above another knot of letters.
This tree, Boy's tree, is cracked
& peeling. Its body is mired
in the branches of the trees around it.

Boy unbuttons his shirt & the scalpel licks
his skin open. He pries apart ribs like a bear trap
& I see his heart arrested. He reaches in,
grabs hold & wrenches it a couple times.
Sounds like a boot meeting mud & I'm afraid
to hold his hand, the scalpel still in it.
Boy's neck muscles tense. Silver thuds
a grounded limb. I pick up the scalpel,
the wrong end. His blood, my blood, our —

SHAPING

When Boy smiles his teeth are tiny black birds
taking flight. The other day a glass broke
in the kitchen sink & the top of my hand went
open. There weren't enough paper towels & I chewed
the stitching for hours, waiting for Boy to notice.
Sometimes I dream my lungs are made of glass
& I have to be very careful. I don't know how
to keep my legs from vibrating. It's work
to find a place to stop & breathe. Then this splitting,
a slow departure: Boy's mouth as a place to launch &
I'm not sure what we're looking for, which words
can make this make sense. We're on the beach
again. His pockets are full of enough metal
to melt & make another sculpture of ourselves.

DREAM

We're on a street neither of us seems to recognize. I let go of Historian's hand & walk into a bakery on the corner. When he gets there I'm aproned behind the counter. When he gets there I'm flipping through a book of birthday themes. When he gets there my face is on the television hung above the cupcakes. Then a shift change, a checkout, a commercial break. Historian cannot find fast enough in his books where I've gone.

THURSDAY EVENING

We are not equipped to do this, to put this body back together. Not with its throat in pieces & its feet missing. Not since the dog ran off with one of the ears & the other is buried between the trees. If only one of us could touch the skin without flinching, could do this without sinking. But Boy's hands are not still or steady enough, & my stomach is always on the verge of emptying. He wonders if focusing on the bones would help, would make this less difficult. If there is a way we could forget that what's in front of us used to be alive & breathing. If we can ignore our surroundings, brown leaves covered in blood, & pretend that we can't smell the body rotting. If it's easier to reconstruct a body this way, with its heart missing. But the body is still the body & it is still here in front of us in pieces. Who will pick the parts from the grass & put them back together. Who will bury the body with its ear between the trees.

RESEARCH

Historian, remember the special collections? They asked us to remove our coats & put your umbrella in a locker. You filled out three separate forms before you were able to look at the manuscripts. I am used to instant gratification. I peruse the aisle at the library & find the book I want & read it standing. Here, the librarian has an assistant make copies. I look for a machine to do it myself & there isn't one. Everything is filtered, Historian. You aren't allowed to take the book from the shelf yourself & you aren't allowed to make your own copies. Part of the joy of handling a book is doing these things. Don't you want to know where the texts sit when you're not looking at them? Don't you want to feel them split & lay flat in your hands as you copy their insides?

DAMAGES

our mouths are empty of teeth & our gums
healed with invisible scars // when we talk
it sounds the same like we never had them

when I ask how we eat Boy says everything is
soft enough everything here adjusts // one day
he wakes without a rib cage & when I press

my mouth into his chest it gives where his bones
should be // he counts & says he'll wait
says he can stay for days until we find them

DREAM

The trees in our backyard are blooming

bullets. All these copper-coated

bits of lead thud the grass & Boy is the grass.

He wakes up with bruises & counts them

in the bathroom mirror. I tell him

I can't see anything. He says right here &

here & here, his last jab surrounded

by a web of freckles. For a moment

Boy seems like a child. For a moment he is.

II

JOURNEY

There is a car & Boy can't decide
which one of us is driving. The radio
keeps repeating the same song, my
favorite, but Boy says it's his,
& I wonder how long we can keep this
up, how long each of us can claim to be
the other. We measure hands against
hands, fingers against fingers, as if knowing
which are larger, bonier, more freckled
is going to solve anything. Boy says
This feels different somehow. Are we
on a different road? Are those the same
trees? I tell Boy I'm not sure, but I'm lying.
I know this is not any different from last week,
last month, last year, when we drove home &
the trees were iced over & swaying in the wind.
The way he looks at me with his hand
too far up my leg & his teeth bursting
from his mouth, I wonder if there is a word
for smiling & feeling sick at the same time,
if there is a way for me to say this. But
the potholes keep appearing too late
& out of nowhere. The car jerks, the tires
dip & for a moment we are both above
& below the ground. In the next, we're just above.

RESURGENCE

Historian says the forest is ripe
with intentional & non-intentional
creatures. Boy digs a trench near
the creek & fills it with dead
squirrels. I ask if they were dead
when he found them. Boy shrugs.
Historian says the squirrels
are non-intentional creatures & we
mark their individual headstones
appropriately. Under Boy's nails
is squirrel blood & dirt & fur.
Historian nods when I mouth
Boy's fingers, sucking the grime.
Historian won't want to kiss me
after this I'm sure. I expect him
to kiss Boy instead, but instead
Historian mouths my fingers.
What he's after I'm not sure.

SETTLING

Boy says we can swim in the hole between the rocks &
pretend they're mountains, pretend the water is the ocean,
pretend the ocean floor is the moon's surface.

There is no way to keep our bodies tethered, he says.
We are free to forget the bones we're missing,
the places where our skin refuses to meet.

DREAM

Boy is a lamp & I'm the wooden table
beneath his body. Somebody keeps setting

a drink on me without using a coaster.
Boy's left on for so long his mouth is

on fire. When he's turned off & somebody
sleeps, my wood starts to settle. Boy's wire

relaxes against my back. In the dark
somebody can't find Boy's switch. In the dark

somebody forgets where its glass of water
is exactly. I absorb the liquid & a small

section of me warps beneath Boy's wire.

BOY BUILDS A CAGE OUT OF BIRD RIBS

He kills a hundred birds to do this. They are tiny birds. Boy uses a lot of glue but I can still smell the meat. The cage is shaped like a phone booth. It is big enough for two people but the sides are fragile. We keep close to each other not to bump into them. Boy's shoulder knocks my chin. My shoulder knocks his chin. Our shoulders & our chins keep meeting each other. I can't raise my arms. I tell Boy I feel trapped. *This is a cage*, he says. *This is how it's supposed to feel.* I ask him where he found all the birds & he says there are trees full of empty nests in the back yard. The crowd of bodies on the carpet shifts. A bird burrows its way out & sits atop the other birds. *Little bastard*, Boy says. The bird watches us & we watch the bird & the bird watches us watch it. Boy runs the back of his hand along his forehead. A streak of red bisects the strip of skin between his eyebrows & his hairline. I try to lick it off & Boy closes his eyes. My elbow unhinges several of the ribs when I put my hand on Boy's back. Almost instantly we're shaking bones out of our hair. Almost instantly Boy's at it with the glue again.

RECOVERY

Historian's hands are full of feathers &
Boy's hands full of rocks, a flanking,
& me wearing my asbestos gloves again.

In front of us a stack of books, each
with a page missing. A scavenger
hunt, our hands knotted in search.

What's been removed, Historian?
What's been misplaced? My hands
are tired but I'm not afraid. Even if

it takes a stretch of years to find,
tell me we won't stop looking,
Historian. Tell me we'll never stop.

GIANTS

Boy is naked & I keep my eyes, a gentleman,
I keep my hands above his waist till his teeth
catch my tongue & our middles crack
in my sheets. His hand fumbles around me.
I notice his eyes notice my eyes & he hauls
his stubble against my collarbone, my jaw.
His lips ground my forehead rare. My bed
steadies his hand & Boy is done. He considers
our stomachs, my face. I nod toward the door,
the towel hung. Boy stumbles & erases me
from his skin, watching his bones as they brighten.

DREAM

My reflection in an array of sharp instruments // Walls &
floor white & licked fluorescent // Over there a bucket of
corn syrup & food coloring // Boy says the chain has a trick
link // Historian says even my crisis thoughts are
nondenominational // Until my hands are free Boy says
he'll let me cut them off // Historian says he'll take us
home & sew us back together // If only I still had that scalpel

BOY IS WINTER'S TONGUE

Boy shows up to the restaurant cradling
a coffee can. He says it's full of ashes,
says he's written every memory
he can think of & burned the papers
in this can. These are the ashes
& he wants me to have them. I ask him
every memory of what. He says every
memory of everything & pushes it over
to my side of the table. He's going
to the bathroom. He'll only be a minute.
Boy doesn't come back & I call him.
I get voicemail. *Hi! You've reached Boy.*
I'm out slaying dragons. I open the can.
It's crowded with blank pieces
of notebook paper. I drive home.
His drawer in my bedroom is gutted.

★

It's snowing for the first time all winter
& Boy knocks on my door. He's grown
a beard. He's wearing my scarf.
He asks me to come outside
& build a snowman. It's four in the morning.
I've just gotten out of the shower.
I say I haven't heard from you,
I don't know where you've been.
He says he's been at the library.

I say you left me a coffee can full of blank
paper. He puts a gloved hand on my belly,
says please come build a snowman.

★

Boy hasn't left my house for days.
He walks around in my jeans & shirts
& reorganizes my books. There's a picture
of the two of us, a snowman between.
Boy asks to sleep face to face. He tells me
about when he was a kid & it rained,
he would race from the porch
to the tire swing in his back yard,
pretending the rain was a portal
& the swing was in a different
dimension. He would listen to his mother
scream at him to come inside. He wouldn't scream
or say anything back. He used to think
about lightning striking the tree. He used
to imagine the bark glowing. I say I like
to think of you swinging, kicking the air
back. No rain, no portal. He says
you can think that if you want to.

★

Boy tells me he fucked someone else
but I shouldn't worry because he's here
& we made a snowman. He tells me

he dreamed about us fucking
in a field of dead sunflowers.
I walk outside & I'm drowning
in a tub full of ice. Boy is behind me
& buries me neck deep in a blanket.
He says in his dream the sunflowers
are black & wrinkled, but the harder
we go the petals start to get their color
back. He says the black falls off
like a snake sheds skin. We get older
when the flowers do this. He looks
at my body, he looks at my face
& it's cracked & my hair is white.
He says we keep fucking until the skin
peels. Our muscles drip off & our organs
pile on the ground. Our bones rasp against
each other. I think of sunflowers yellow
like jaundice getting caught in his spine.

★

We're watching television. Boy's watching
& I'm reading in the same room. I excuse
myself to fix a drink & come back
with the knife Boy's mother gave us
for Christmas last year. Boy's body
is on the couch. I stand behind him,
place my right hand on his shoulder.
He tilts his head up & my left hand
shoves the blade between his ribs.
It's quick. It happens before his face
forgets his indifference. Later I wash

Boy off in the shower. I step out,
wet feet wary of the polished
tile, & steel my palms against
the sink. Brushing my teeth I see
Boy in the mirror. He holds the knife.
He hands it to me. He asks me to do it again.

ITERATIONS

I don't know why we keep coming back to this forest.
Boy has buried all the squirrels. Historian already
figured out all the paths we could possibly take to get
to the creek. Each of us has drank from the creek
& bathed in the creek & pissed in the creek. We have
left our mark & I'm not sure why we're not leaving.
Boy finds a spot beneath a tree & stretches out
taking up half of the forest floor. Historian & I
have to keep stepping over Boy's limbs & sometimes
we step into each other, a pile of Boy & Historian & me.
Makes me nauseous how we smell like geraniums losing
their nectar, our skin leaving, our sweetness waning,
& I know I have been here before. I have been here
so many times. I am tired of my uneasy stomach.

ROUTINE

All day long Boy's body is bent over carcasses. Our house is littered with charts & drawings & the remains of unidentified humans. Boy says he doesn't understand his body, the way it's put together, how it snaps into place. I think about telling him that he can learn from my body, but I don't. Instead I ask if he's going to be at this much longer. Instead I walk around the house naked because I'm not above coercion. His shirt is sweaty against my skin. His hands are licked with bone dust & when he palms my belly I taste chalk. He counts the number of times he locks our front door before he goes to sleep. He counts the number of times he checks to make sure all the burners on the stove are off before he slides his body next to mine. He tries to synchronize our breathing, but rolls over when I won't quit stopping.

EXPIRATION DATE

The bedroom floor is littered with beheaded marigolds & Boy is wearing that thing I like which is just his skin but it's broken out in new tattoos. A fish with a cracked mouth gnaws his right hip. A red star approximates his heart. What I mistake for candles around the room are hollowed-out flashlights, their insides paper-stuffed & on fire. Boy gets up from the bed & starts dumping the flashlights on the floor. He says *Did you forget to grab the shovel?* The smell of marigolds burning smells a lot like the places where Boy's skin meets itself. Bitter. Sweet. Unbearable. He says *I told you we were going to need the shovel.* The smoke alarm isn't beeping yet. *I told you*, he says.

COLLECTION

Boy is a pile of photographs, sand & dirt stuck to his faces. Historian says I should start a catalog. He says I'm always misinterpreting Boy & that I have to get it right this time. He hands me a shoebox full of blank paper & says documentation is the first step. I ask *The first step to what?* but Historian doesn't answer. He wanders off into the kitchen & comes back with a knife, says *here, you can start with this.*

MEAT CUTE

Boy unzips his skin
& tells me to turn
back around,

to look at his
pretty red flesh,
press my fingers

& watch it give.
He asks me what
my blood type is.

He asks if I'm attached
to my body. I'm not
sure. I say I don't think

we should be here.
He says please
give me your

hands & holds his
out. I say these
aren't my hands.

SAFETY

There is an ongoing debate
about the kitchen window.
Boy insists on keeping
the shutters open. But again
the outside lights aren't working.
It's difficult at night to see
what's in the yard & I have
a vivid imagination. Boy says
the yard is open, vacant. He says
you worry too much about nothing.

DREAM

Our legs are stilts. Beyond our ankles
are the blunt ends of crutches. Our feet
are missing. But our hands are fine,
Boy says. There's a rope suspended
between our bodies. Our wooden knees
are disappearing. In dirt. In asphalt. In sand.
It changes. Branches held aloft, moss
tonguing our shoulders. Houses on either
side, miles of chainlink mixed with picket
& punctuated by light poles. An ocean
with its margin specked by snapped shells.
Boy asks me what I feel like doing
& before I answer his stilts are discarded
in the shells. His body disappears
& reappears in the green of the ocean.

BOY SITS AT THE DINING ROOM TABLE

& with his right hand he drops a hammer on each fingernail. I say *How was your day, sweetheart*? He doesn't look up. He watches the hammer fall.

★

& with his right hand he drops a hammer on each fingernail. I say *How was your day, sweetheart*? He looks up. The hammer hangs slack in his hand. *It was fine* he says. *How was yours?*

★

& with his right hand he drops a hammer on each fingernail. I say *How was your day, sweetheart*? He doesn't look up. The hammer disappears. His hands look useless without it.

★

& with his right hand he drops a hammer on each fingernail. I say *How was your day, sweetheart*? He looks up, stands. Raises the hammer to our china cabinet.

★

& with his right hand he drops a hammer on each fingernail. I say *How was your day, sweetheart*? He looks up. The hammer leaves his hand in my direction.

★

& with his right hand he drops a hammer on each fingernail. I say *How was your day, sweetheart*? He looks down. He expects his fingernails to be black with bruises. They are unharmed, perfect.

DENIAL

Blood is tumbling out of Boy's mouth & behind him
I'm pressing my teeth against his shoulder hoping
it will stop soon. I wonder if Historian thinks
I'm being dishonest. I wonder if my dreams make me
dishonest. My hands have been in Boy's blood
so many times I'm almost comforted by it. I'm afraid
to say this to Boy in my dream. I'm afraid
to wake up Historian & tell him about Boy & Boy's blood,
about my teeth against his shoulder & how easily
our bodies snap into place in my head. I'm not
unaware of the juxtaposition of violence & quiet,
what it means or if it means anything. I'm not sure
if the violence is our bodies snapping into place
& the quiet is the tumbling blood or if I'm
getting things wrong again. Boy's face keeps changing
either way. I wake up Historian but I'm just shaking
a pillow that Historian's face is fading from.
If Historian is in my bathroom I can't hear him
& if he's in my house I can't smell him.

THIS POSSIBLE LIFE

I trace our cuts again. Time beneath

each other's hands. A heap of sound.

Streets all fluttering. Boy walks

ahead of me always. He can't

remember if he changed the sheets.

He says his hands are cold. A broken

window. How long will it take

him to notice. We arrive in the middle

of the movie & stitch. There are only

so many days I can wear the same face.

INVENTION

I am trying to figure out how I got here & where
here is. The bathroom door keeps shutting itself.
None of my hairs are the same length. Boy is
nowhere to be found & everywhere smells like you.
You tell me you're not a replacement & I believe you,
I want to believe you. But something is wrong
with my eyes & their seeing. Historian, your face
all blurred. My ears are still broken from the blast &
can't you try putting your mouth closer to the phone
or maybe closer to my neck. I am tired of asking
for more volume. I am tired of asking for more words.

DREAM

Historian keeps unmaking & making the bed, trying the pillows in different positions, wishing the sheets different colors & watching them change. Boy rearranges the living room & moves the television into the hall closet. He says we're all going to read now & he hands Historian & me old volumes of poetry written in French, except none of us can read the language that well. Boy begins to write his favorite words on the wall in black marker & Historian searches for a dictionary but can't find it. I tell Boy I can only recognize *oui* & *jour* & *oeil*. I tell Historian the yeses, the days, & the eyes.

TRAVEL

Historian, a cage where my chest
should be. Inside it: metal lungs,
a wooden heart that tastes like oak.
Cut in half to see how old I am,
all results are inconclusive. Guess
who can't count tree rings.
I must've missed that year.

★

Surrounded by doubled-over pines,
I can't see beyond their needles
on the ground, their needles licking
my arms, their needles hanging on.
Historian, my hands all opened.
Take them please before the wind.

★

The light posts are candle-shaped
& their bulbs have flames inside.
Technology eclipsing itself,
forgetting its history, Historian.
One of us should write this down.

★

The moss here is probably older
than we are. Waving at us, it's hard
to know whether it's saying goodbye
or hello. Are we arriving or leaving,
Historian? Quickest Answer. Go.

IV

RELOCATION

Boy says I want to give you something
circular & he pulls a broken compass

from his backpocket. He sets the silver
in my hand & says let's live in a new town

without bridges or guns, anything that reminds
him of all the ways I've tried to kill him.

He says you can wear those boots you like,
our backyard's wooded & we'll take turns

burying cold rocks & wash each other's hair
to pry the dirt from under our fingernails.

He'll buy fresh fruit & after sex he'll peel
an orange, shove the flesh into his mouth

& sitting close, my teeth sore from grinding
when we're sleeping, the acid scalds my eyes.

DREAM

Boy dies & masked men in black coats take away his skin & his organs. They give me his bones in a box & I string them up as windchimes, hang some on the front porch & some on the back. Every morning I check for the newspaper that doesn't arrive & Boy's bones clatter a beautiful hello. I can't sleep so I step out back to hear the crickets. His bones are silent & I flick one just to watch it knock into the others.

TO & FROM

I am tired of when I touch you your center is the first place I go. My hands are so tiny, all disproportionate & I am afraid of their memories. Do you remember the black & gold bowl & the cherry varnished hardwood? The rupture between our feet. A punctuation. A scattering.

⋆ ⋆ ⋆

We said we'd never talk about blood again. How hard it is to wash out of my white shirts. How neither of us can get the taste out of our mouths. Remember my body falling from the roof, my knee giving, your boot at the back of my leg. Remember when our couch went up in flames. Remember our burning faces.

⋆ ⋆ ⋆

I don't know which set of bones will atrophy first, skull or rib cage. The end of each approaching. I am dramatic, remember. I am paranoid. I am anxious. I am trying to find my leftover Xanax & I wish you would quit thwarting the mission. Quit plunging elbow deep into cheap black hats pulling out dead rabbits. You are no magician. Put down the saw.

⋆ ⋆ ⋆

I'm not sure why you keep asking me to meet you here. I mean, I get it—the leftover holes in the ground are a metaphor. The swingset folded into itself behind the shed is your childhood. I'm not the bluntest knife in the drawer, you know. But why you come here is a mystery. This place you can't seem to shake.

★ ★ ★

I know that we've been here before. The physical here. The you-asking-me-why-we're-here here. I keep expecting the swingset to shift, to relocate. I keep expecting the holes to fill themselves. I keep expecting you to stop coming with me.

★ ★ ★

I'm tired of waking up with marks I can't explain. I have five sets of dental records around my ribs, a few on either shoulder, a couple on my left hip. I already know you don't remember. I already know you're not going to stop anytime soon. Maybe you can tell me if you have a number in mind.

★ ★ ★

It's you trying to make sense of things that always gets us into trouble. Trying to put things into order. Trying to discern. It's you trying too hard. The way you pull every book from the shelf. The way you search for reason even if it's nowhere to be found.

* * *

I'm pretty good at discerning. About as good as you are at dismantling. About as good as you are at creating situations & not walking away from them until it's too late to walk. About as good as you are at introducing violence & being surprised when it shows up again.

* * *

You keep putting memories in the wrong order. You keep switching our hands & I'm not sure which of us did what anymore. There's not much difference between a scalpel & a knife when you really think about it. There's not much difference between keeping a coffee can full of empty paper & burying photographs in the front yard.

* * *

Things get complicated when you decide my body is your body. You unhook my brain & snap yours into place & it's not the best fit. Sometimes there's a lot of blood in the spaces your brain knocks when you're moving me around. Remember that our blood types aren't compatible. Remember my brain has a shelf life. Remember my skull is bigger than yours.

* * *

You never used to worry so much about the way we fit together. I mean, I've gotten used to bleeding a little. I'm okay with being uncomfortable if it means you're still here. I don't think so much about shelf life. I guess that's where you & I are different.

PREPARATION

Boy has a particular heart & he's turning it over in his hands like an object he's trying to comprehend. It's like his heart is an artifact & Boy's memorizing its intricacies because he has to complete a report based entirely on his findings. He picks a dash of bone & I add it to the other bits collected in the forgotten glass of water on my nightstand. I'm trying to be patient but outside the snow is dissolving. Outside the sun's erasing everything & inside Boy's poring over something I don't really want to understand. I think about his bones sunk in the glass, how they confetti the water, & I drink them as a distraction. Boy continues to thumb his heart, this misshapen ornament slow-leaking in all directions. A bone catches in my throat. I choke.

CONFLATION

Boy & Historian & me all tangled up
in each other. What are we doing?
Why is neither of them breathing?
Boy's ribs are shifting again & those are
Historian's hands in Boy's chest.
I'm jealous. I'm not sure I'm jealous
because Historian is in Boy's chest
& not mine or if I'm jealous because
those are Historian's hands & not mine.
Why are we reducible to blood,
where it is & where it isn't? I want
to throw one of them down & fuck him.
Wait. I'm self-shrinking again. Replace fuck
with leave. Replace throw with hold.
Replace want with have. Replace I with
Historian. Replace one of them with me.

TIME STAMP

It's a Thursday. We're at the heart
sharpening store & Boy has no memory
of me. In one corner there is
a woman with a scalpel. In the other,
a man running a white machine.

The machine has a slot for hearts
& several flashing buttons. In the back
a suited woman sells refurbished
memories. A sign reads *Not For The*
Feint of Heart & neither of us laugh

at the pun. Boy has forgotten pun,
perhaps. His hand is cuffing my wrist,
his eyes wandering the store.
The suited woman's assistant is naked,
but nobody seems to notice. His hands carry

jars full of multicolored air. The suited
woman has a machine too. Except hers is
red & there is only one button & it doesn't
flash. There is a hole big enough for a jar's
mouth & the assistant fits the jars one by

one. The multicolored air is in the machine
for a moment before the suited woman pushes
the button—the suited woman is distracted
by Boy. I'm not sure if it's his hand shackling
my wrist or his blankness or both. Her finger

lingers above the button. There are other
people in line ahead of us. We are stuck
for moments that way, Boy's hand around
my wrist, the suited woman's finger cocked,
the line of customers between us & her.

DREAM

Boy says he's looking for a place to hide our clothes
again, another spot to make a hole. He lifts his shirt &
points to a thousand daisies waiting to be plucked. I say
I'm tired of everything always turning into something else.
I'm tired of the way he keeps making himself impossible to ignore.
Boy says *You only come here because it's easy*
& before I can say that isn't true, the flowers start
disappearing. Boy is just his skin again, deathly
white & scarred around his ribs. His hair & fingernails are
longer than they should be. I say *This is another dream,*
isn't it? & Boy says *If only we were sleeping.*

DENOUEMENT

Historian's body & Boy's body & my body
& all of them not moving, all splayed & split
open. Yellow flowers again. A patch of goldenrods
pinned down by our weight. I don't feel like watching
our bodies reanimate & the flowers die. Boy says
think of our bodies as an installation. An institution—
an indictment, an insurrection. Or, let's be honest:
an inconvenience. He says we're taking up too much
space again. We're a distraction. We're an obstruction.
I say who's going to get rid of us? I'm tired of waiting
to be hauled off & buried. I don't like the way
Boy smells anymore. I take back the double plot
at the cemetery. Historian makes a prediction
based on previous occurrences & estimates
that we'll be found in approximately six days.
I've never wanted Historian to be more wrong,
but he tells me to be patient. I close my eyes
but nothing shifts. Historian's standing over me, handing
me Boy's hands, saying here, Boy left these for you.

DREAM

Boy is asking for a box full of hurry
his arms angled up & his teeth

those goddamned white teeth of his
are turning red & when did my ear

make its way into his mouth & when
did his forehead start scrolling *please*

if both ears are attached still
then who is Boy chewing on & whose

voice keeps echoing *it's time* & Boy's
mouth isn't moving & Boy's mouth isn't

chewing & that's not Boy's mouth
I've been staring at not Boy's face even

ACKNOWLEDGMENTS

Many thanks to the editors of the following publications in which some of these poems first appeared, sometimes in slightly different form: *alice blue review, Copper Nickel, Corium, DIAGRAM, H_NGM_N, Heavy Feather Review, Hobart, ILK Journal, > kill author, METAZEN, New England Review, Real Poetik, Sixth Finch, Smokelong Quarterly,* & *Split Lip Magazine.*

Special thanks to Lisa Tallin for her feedback, support, & amazing friendship, & for such a beautiful cover image; to Matthew Mahaney for reading & rereading from beginning to end; to Darby K. Price for her encouragement & support from each end of the country; to Josh Buckner for being there; to Zach, my mom, pop, & dad for their love & support.

Many thanks to my teachers & classmates in the MFA program at the University of Alabama for reading & commenting on many of these poems. Thanks especially to Peter Streckfus-Green, E K Carpenter, Casey Fagan, & Farren Stanley.

A barrel of thanks to C. Dale Young for believing in my work & coming up with such a fitting title for this book; to Sabrina Orah Mark for a beautiful blurb that brings tears to my eyes; to Matthew Olzmann for digging in & being the best sounding board; to Dzanc Books for putting my book into the world.

Borrowings:

The epigraph is from Sylvia Plath's "The Arrival of the Bee Box." Historian's name was partially inspired by Matthea Harvey's "TERROR OF THE FUTURE / 10." "This Possible Life" borrows two-thirds of its title from a line in Jack Gilbert's "Going There." The title for "Boy Is Winter's Tongue" is a reimagining of a line from Matthew Rohrer's "The Amaranth."